WISLEY HANDBOOK 24

Bulbs indoors

A. G. L. HELLYER

LONDON
The Royal Horticultural Society
1976

Contents

Section I. Cultivation. *page*

1. The charm of bulbs — 3
2. Qualities and limitations — 3
3. Soils and containers — 5
4. The importance of warmth and cold — 9
5. Feeding — 11
6. Pests and diseases — 12

Section II. Recommended Kinds

Alphabetical list — 13

Photos: Ernest Crowson

Printed in England by
Henry Stone & Son (Printers) Ltd., Swan Close, Banbury, Oxfordshire

Section I. Cultivation

1. The Charm of Bulbs

There is something about a bulb which makes it attractive even in its dry state. It is nice to handle and good to look at, fat and full of promise of pleasure to come. The very fact that most bulbs can be taken out of the soil for a time and kept dry makes them easy to market or to despatch over long distances at a minimum of risk and expense.

Many bulb flowers are exceptionally beautiful in form and some have a brilliance of colour and a glistening petal quality which add greatly to their attractiveness. And to all these qualities some also add fragrance, on occasion so rich and penetrating as to surpass that of most other flowers and even to be a little overpowering in enclosed places.

Another notable virtue is that a good bulb not only holds enough stored food to allow it to grow for a considerable time with no other help than water, warmth and light, but quite often it contains an embryo flower ready to develop to full size and beauty as soon as conditions are right. That is why bulbs such as hyacinths and daffodils are first class beginner's plants. Provided they are given just a little commonsense treatment it is virtually impossible to go wrong with them in the first year. One such success at the outset can be good for morale and just the thing to create confidence to go on to more difficult plants.

But it is important to remember that the bulbs were able to give that easy success because they had been well grown the year before they were purchased. If they are to go on multiplying and flowering year after year it is essential to see that the original stored energy is replaced annually. This is where the real test of skill comes in growing bulbs.

2. Qualities and Limitations

The term 'house plant' has come to be applied to any plant that will survive for a long time indoors, whether it be in a living room, office or shop. Since the light in such places is nearly always much lower in intensity than outdoors and the atmosphere is usually drier, the range of plants suitable is limited and for the less well lit places is virtually confined to foliage plants.

In this sense bulbs are not good house plants. They are nearly all grown for their flowers, which usually only last for a few weeks, few of them have really attractive foliage, many being positively untidy when out of flower, and quite a lot die right down and are out of sight for several months each year. Most need a good deal of light and quite a number must have sunshine if they are to go on growing well year after year.

Because they are not good house plants in the current use of that term it does not mean that quite a lot of bulbs are not good plants to have indoors at certain periods. But those periods should be limited, and it will help a great deal and enable a much wider range of bulbs to be grown if some other simple accommodation is available when they are not actually coming into flower and flowering. For much of the year even a balcony or a flat roof is better than a room and if a yard or garden is available the range of possibilities is even greater. Further horizons will be opened if a sun-room, glazed verandah, conservatory or greenhouse is available. Then there is really no limit to the bulbous plants that can be enjoyed, to be brought indoors for a few weeks while they are at their most interesting and beautiful and then to be returned to ideal growing conditions. However, without any of these aids, it is possible to grow quite a number of bulbs indoors, giving them the sunniest windows when they are in growth and then perhaps packing them away in a cupboard when they die down, to take the annual rest which is part of the life cycle of most, but not all, of them.

First, exactly what does one mean by a bulb? Technically it is a storage organ composed of overlapping fleshy scales, rather like a very large, fat growth bud. In some kinds, such as hyacinths and tulips, the scales are so closely packed as to appear almost solid, in others, such as some lilies, they are quite loose and easily broken off. However the bulb is formed, its purpose is the same, to store food and moisture. Many bulbous plants come from regions where the climate is hot and dry in summer, but cool or even cold and moist in winter. Some have acquired the habit of growing when other plants are at rest and then dying down and becoming dormant for a few weeks or months when the competition above ground is too great. These are the winter or spring flowering kinds, and because they flower so early they have learned to manage without strong sunlight, at least for a good deal of their growing period, though some have quite a high light requirement for the last few weeks before they die down. This ability to grow in a relatively low light intensity does help them to adapt to room conditions where the light intensity, even in a sunny window, is never as high as outdoors, though it does also mean that they may need to be removed to a warmer, sunnier place after they have flowered.

A few bulbs never do become really dormant, but retain some leaves all the year. All these differences make it impossible to generalise about treatment, least of all about watering, since some bulbs can be kept quite dry and even out of soil for months, whereas others must be kept growing gently even when they are resting. It is all these differences, in addition to their great range of flower forms and colours that make them such fascinating plants to grow.

But there are also some plants in this book which are not bulbs at all. My reason for including them is that they behave in a similar way to bulbs, are purchased from the same sources and are commonly included in bulb catalogues and bulb books.

What they all share in common is some kind of storage organ which may be a corm or a tuber when it is not a true bulb. Corms really are solid tissue throughout, except for a dry membraneous outer coat, two familiar examples being the gladiolus and the crocus. Tubers can be swollen stems or roots, like the tuberous rooted begonias and gloxinia and cyclamen.

If you are simply interested in growing plants there is no need to remember any of these things, but it is nice to know the answers when someone says that terms are being used wrongly.

The best time to start with bulbs, corms or tubers is towards the end of their resting season, if they have one, that is just before they are ready to start into growth again. Spring flowering bulbs, such as daffodils, hyacinths and tulips, rest in summer and so are planted in late summer or autumn. Summer-flowering gladioli rest in winter and so are planted in spring, but there are also kinds which make their growth in winter, flower in spring or early summer and then rest, and these must be planted in autumn. So there is no one time of year to buy bulbs and their allies, and the work of potting can be spread over many months.

Like other plants bulbs may be hardy, half-hardy or tender. 'Hardy' means that they will stand quite a lot of frost and can be grown outdoors in most (maybe all) parts of Britain. 'Half-hardy' means that they will not survive more than a few degrees of frost, perhaps none at all, but can be grown outdoors in summer in most parts of Britain, since there is unlikely to be severe or prolonged frost between early June and late September. 'Tender' means that they are not really happy outdoors in Britain at any time except perhaps in a few very warm and sheltered places, since it is not simply frost that harms them but low temperatures such as we frequently experience even in summer.

Of course if bulbs are to be grown indoors all the time these differences do not matter greatly, but, as I have already explained, it is usually convenient, and often good for the plants, to stand them outside at certain periods, and before doing so one must know whether this is safe and, if so, at what time of year. Instructions about this are included for all the individual kinds recommended in this book.

3. Soils and Containers

Outdoors it is not too difficult to give bulbs the right conditions to go on thriving and flowering more or less indefinitely, though some kinds are a good deal more exacting than others. Indoors it is less easy to get conditions just right, which is one reason why the advice is so often given that bulbs should only be grown once inside and then either thrown away or planted outdoors. But that can make bulb growing quite expensive, and one of the things I shall be trying to show in this book is how at least some bulbs can be kept in good condition in pots for a very long time.

The worst way to grow bulbs if you are hoping to keep them for a number of years is in the special bulb glasses which are filled only with water and maybe a few pieces of charcoal. This is a fascinating way to grow hyacinths, especially for children. It is also an easy way because once the glasses have been filled to the correct level and one bulb placed in each expanded neck (specially shaped to receive it), there is really very little to do except to put the glass in the lightest possible place and top up the water occasionally to keep it just fractionally below the base of the bulb. When the leaves start to grow and the flower stem appears it also helps to give the pot a quarter turn every day so that it slowly goes round and round and each side gets equal illumination. It is also better if the glass is coloured (most of the special bulb glasses are) as this restricts the amount of light reaching the water and so checks the growth of algae, which discolour and foul the water. But that is all there is to it, and on a sunny window ledge hyacinths can be planted in September and be in flower by February or even earlier if a start is made with specially prepared bulbs.

But that is another story to which I shall return later. The point I want to stress here is that bulbs grown in water are unable to replenish their food stores sufficiently to give a repeat performance the next year. Of course one could put a little plant food in the water, which is a simplified form of the method of cultivation known as hydroponics, but then one has to be very careful to get the chemicals and the quantities just right and that changes a simple system into a much more complex one. So normally the hyacinth in the glass has to manage on water alone and that is a starvation diet if one is looking beyond the first year result.

So, though bulb glasses are fun, if you really want to grow bulbs indoors seriously and in variety, you have to be prepared to use soil or a soil substitute. Exactly what is selected will depend partly on convenience, partly on the kind of container used. There are two basic types of container, drained and undrained. Ordinary flower pots and half or dwarf pots (which are a little less deep and excellent for small bulbs and corms) are of the first type, most ornamental bowls of the second.

What makes this so important is that it is difficult to keep soil in good condition in containers that have no outlet for surplus water. One can help a little by watering very carefully and adding plenty of coarse sand and peat to the soil to keep it porous, and also by mixing in some crushed charcoal to absorb acids formed in the soil, or crushed shell to neutralise them. But none of these precautions will prevent the air being driven out if too much water is given, and roots without air in the soil die of drowning. But all this is making unnecessary difficulties and if one wishes to use some kind of soil or peat potting compost it is far and away best to choose properly drained containers. But then water will run out of the drainage holes at times (after all that is what they are there for) so instead of standing the pots directly on furniture or on window ledges, stand each pot in a saucer (special saucers can be obtained) or arrange several pots in a plant stand.

If, however, you opt for undrained containers, perhaps ornamental bowls of some kind, you should forget about potting composts and use bulb fibre. This can be purchased ready for use and may vary in constituents according to the manufacturer who has prepared it, but if you prefer to make your own a good mixture is 6 parts (by bulk) of sphagnum peat, 2 parts of crushed oyster shell and one part of crushed charcoal. Any convenient unit can be used, e.g. a tea cup, old tin or pint measure. All the ingredients must be thoroughly mixed and then well moistened, which may take quite a time because dry peat resists water, though once it is moist it absorbs water like a sponge. Even if ready mixed bulb fibre is purchased it is likely to be too dry and will need to be thoroughly moistened before use. One way to do this is to put it in a large bowl or bucket, pour water over it and mix it around, then leave it for an hour or so and repeat the watering and mixing, continuing in this way until it feels nicely moist without being soggy.

The drawback to bulb fibre is that, like the water in the bulb glasses, it contains little plant food. It is there mainly to support the bulbs and roots and supply them with moisture, which it does very well, but when the bulbs have completed their growth they are unlikely to have fattened up sufficiently to flower again the following year. So they must either be thrown away or planted in good rich soil out of doors.

For any kind of permanancy potting composts are the answer, and here there is a wide choice of both soil and soilless types. In Britain the most popular soil composts are made to the John Innes formulae and are based on loam, peat and sand in the bulk proportions 7, 3 and 2.

Loam is a rather vague term for natural soil containing clay, sand and humus. A medium loam is specified, i.e. neither too light and sandy nor too heavy and full of clay, preferably prepared from rotted turves and slightly acid (pH 6.3). Even that is not a very precise description, but if you have access to what seems to be good quality soil it will probably do just as well as most of the so-called 'loam' used by manufacturers of John Innes compost. The loam must be sterilised to control soil-borne diseases. The peat should be a good horticultural grade sphagnum peat, the sand coarse and gritty, not sea-shore sand which may contain salt and lime.

John Innes composts also contain fertilisers; a John Innes base fertiliser which can be purchased ready mixed or can be made at home with 2 parts superphosphate, 2 parts hoof and horn meal and 1 part sulphate of potash, all parts this time *by weight*. The ingredients are well mixed, and then measured quantities, plus measured quantities of either ground chalk or ground limestone, are added to the soil, peat and sand mixture. How much of each is added depends upon which John Innes mixture one wishes to use. JIP1 has 4 oz. of base fertiliser and $\frac{3}{4}$ oz. of ground chalk or limestone per bushel. Nos. 2 and 3 composts have twice or three times these quantities of fertiliser, and these are chiefly used for greenhouse plants as the plants get bigger. For most bulbs I think it is best to stick to JIP 1 and give any extra food required by liquid feeding when the plants are in growth.

Because loam is so difficult to define and so hard to find, there has been a continuous development of soilless composts based on peat plus fertilisers, and sometimes also with sand, vermiculite, Perlite or something else to prevent it becoming soggy. There are numerous proprietary brands, all of secret formulation, and I do not think it is very wise to experiment with homemade mixtures. But in America, where a lot of work has been done, especially at the University of California, what are known as the U.C. soil mixes are popular. One that is suitable for bulbs is prepared with equal parts by bulk medium grade sphagnum peat and fine sand to every 20 litres (roughly 5 gallons) of which is added $\frac{1}{4}$ oz. nitrate of potash, $\frac{1}{8}$ oz. sulphate of potash, $1\frac{1}{4}$ oz. superphosphate, $\frac{5}{8}$ oz. finely powdered magnesium limestone and $1\frac{1}{4}$ oz. gypsum. It is most important that all these ingredients are thoroughly mixed. In this context 'fine sand' is defined as grading in particle size from 0.05mm to 0.5mm. This mixture can be stored for quite a long time. It has little reserve plant food and so bulbs grown in it will need extra feeding while in growth. A richer mixture with a greater food reserve can be made with the same proportions of peat and fine sand, but with the addition to every 20 litres of $1\frac{1}{2}$ oz. of either hoof and horn meal or dried blood, $\frac{1}{4}$ oz. nitrate of potash, $\frac{1}{4}$ oz. sulphate of potash, $\frac{1}{2}$ oz. superphosphate, 4 oz. magnesium limestone and $1\frac{1}{2}$ oz. of ground chalk. This mixture should be used within a week of preparation.

Soil composts have the merit of being fairly solid and so giving roots a good hold and preventing plants from toppling over as they get taller and heavier. They also hold plant food well, and are easy to water even when they have been allowed to get too dry.

Soilless composts are light, clean and easy to handle and are usually free of harmful organisms, but the added nutrients are used up rather rapidly, do not support plants so well and can be exceedingly difficult to re-moisten once they dry out, though the U.C. mix described above is better than most in both these last features. The tendency nowadays is towards soilless composts, but my own view is that beginners are likely to find plants easier to handle in 'old fashioned' soil composts. There is, of course, no reason why one should not use both (I certainly do), but they require slightly different management. When potting bulbs (or for that matter any other plants) in soil composts the mixture should be pressed in quite firmly with the fingers. When using soilless composts very little pressure should be used and two or three sharp raps of the container on a bench or other firm surface is sufficient to settle the compost in.

Soilless composts usually dry out more rapidly than soil composts and it is a little more difficult to tell whether they are in need of water. But that is something soon learned with experience. Plastic pots retain their water better than clay pots, but in the dry atmosphere of a living room it is sometimes an advantage to have the air around the pot moist from evaporation, even if this means more frequent watering.

4. The Importance of Warmth and Cold

Many bulbs, but not all, have adapted themselves to grow in awkward climates, usually climates that are hot and dry in summer and moist, cool or positively cold in winter. They have developed subtle mechanisms to deal with these great changes, so that in the wild they respond to the adverse conditions by initiating their flower buds, dying down and becoming semi-dormant and are then ready to start growing again when conditions are right.

When they are grown in gardens, and still more when they are grown indoors, bulbs with this periodic kind of growth must receive the right signals at the right times or they may go completely awry. In the late spring or early summer this is not too difficult since it is increasing sunlight and warmth that tells them to die down, and though our British summers are unlikely to be either as hot or as sunny as those to which they are accustomed, they are usually good enough to set things going, especially if the bulbs are placed in a sunny sheltered place.

What is far more likely to be missing when bulbs are grown indoors is the cold period which some kinds must have before they are ready to grow normally again. In the wild they measure the length of this cold—usually to be regarded as any temperature of about $9°$ C or less—and not until a safe number of weeks have passed (unlikely to be less than twelve and possibly as many as sixteen) will they push shoots above the soil again, though in the meantime they may have made quite a lot of roots.

So it is no use keeping bulbs that have this cold requirement in a warm room or greenhouse all the time. It will simply upset their timing mechanism and make them behave in an abnormal way, perhaps starting to grow without any roots at all, and then collapsing, or growing a little and then losing their flower stems. A lot of the troubles that are put down to all manner of other causes are really due to the bulbs having had an inadequate period of cold or an irregular sequence of cold and warmth before they are made to grow again.

It is possible to give some bulbs their cold treatment while they are out of the ground in summer and this is the way tulips and narcissi are prepared for early forcing. They have been kept for a specified number of weeks at scientifically determined temperatures and so, when planted in late summer or early autumn, behave as if they had already gone through either part or the whole of a winter. Such bulbs may need to be kept a little longer in the cool or they may be ready to go straight into a growing temperature of 13 to 18°C., depending on the way in which they have been prepared. Those sold in the shops are always of the former type, but they do not need as long in the cool, after they have been put into soil, as bulbs which have been stored at normal summer temperatures.

Sometimes the artificial cold treatment is preceded by an artificial warm period immediately the bulbs are lifted, to hasten the formation of flower buds within the bulbs. Hyacinths sold as specially prepared for early flowering are likely to have had heat treatment only and therefore need the whole of their cold treatment after they have been purchased and planted. But what I want to emphasize here is that these pre-treatments in store require expert knowledge of the response, not only of different kinds of bulbs, but even of different varieties of the same kind. They also require accurate control of temperatures. The pre-treatment of hyacinths, for example, may require four changes of temperature precisely timed and controlled. It is not work that can be undertaken in the house, so if 'prepared' bulbs are required they must be purchased, and if retained for flowering in later years must be treated normally.

Real problems can arise indoors if there is no outside place in which bulbs with a periodic habit of growth can be grown for the first 12 to 16 weeks. Remember that it is a temperature of 9°C or less that is usually required. Few rooms, even unheated ones, are much below 13°C in September and October and even in November and December 9°C is very chilly for a house.

Even outdoors it is unlikely that sufficient natural cold will come before mid-October, but gardeners make artificial cold by the simple method of evaporation, the system our grandmothers used for cooling butter. They stand the containers outdoors in the coolest place available, preferably facing north and completely cut off from direct sunshine, and they then cover them to a depth of 3 or 4 inches with damp peat, leaf mould or sand. As the moisture evaporates from this it takes away heat, so lowering the temperature around the bulbs.

It may be possible to do something similar in a yard, on a balcony or in a garage or cellar. It is unlikely that a cupboard in a spare room, so often recommended as a place for starting bulbs, will be sufficiently cool all the time to be really effective before mid-winter. Let me emphasise that cool treatment is not essential for all bulbs, nor do some even have a resting period. I do not know of any corm or tuber that requires cool treatment before it can grow in a normal way, though it would not surprise me if there are some. In the notes on the cultivation of individual species I will make it clear where cool treatment is required and for how long.

5. Feeding

Any plants growing in containers are likely to run short of food before the end of the growing season and this applies just as much to bulbs as it does to plants with no storage systems. When they do this will depend a great deal on the kind of compost in which they are grown. If it is a John Innes type mixture they may keep going happily for several months and need little or no extra feeding, whereas most soilless composts are likely to become exhausted after eight or ten weeks of active growth. With a few exceptions, which are noted in the instructions for individual kinds, it is better to err on the side of starting to feed a little too soon than a little too late, as once a plant gets checked by starvation it is often difficult to get it going again. A rough guide can be the first appearance of flower stems, for this is the time when a plant needs the most food. From then until the foliage begins to show signs of yellowing and dying down, food can usually be given about once every 7 to 10 days, but it must be well diluted and applied direct to the compost, not splashed all over the plant, unless you decide to use a foliar feed which I do not greatly recommend for bulbs.

The simplest and most satisfactory method is to use a concentrated liquid fertiliser specially made for pot plants, and dilute it a little more than recommended by the makers. It is a good idea to use at least two different brands, maybe one based on seaweed another purely on chemicals, since this way the bulbs are likely to get everything they require. It is nitrogen, phosphorus and potash that are most likely to be required, and provided the bulbs are in good compost there should be no need for expensive extras like 'trace elements' and chelated (sequestrated) chemicals. It is only outdoors in awkward soils that deficiencies of this kind sometimes need to be rectified.

As in any pot plant the soil must be moist before feeding occurs, and must never be allowed to become too dry afterwards or the roots may be killed by the concentrated solution.

6. Pests and Diseases

Bulbs and their allies do not suffer greatly from pests when they are grown indoors, though outside they may be attacked by mice, voles and occasionally rats. It is often wise to wire in a bulb plunging bed, using a fine meshed, plastic-covered netting and burying this into the soil as well as covering the top.

Indoors greenflies sometimes appear almost as soon as the shoots are visible and these have probably hatched from eggs laid within the covering scales at the neck of the bulb at the time the foliage was dying down. There are plenty of good greenfly killers, including resmethrin which is safe and does not smell unpleasantly. In the dry air of a house thrips thrive once they get in, but as they are only likely to be brought in during the summer the danger is not great. They are small and very active insects which suck the sap out of leaves and petals, leaving the leaves a highly distinctive grey mottled colour and the flowers blotchy. Gladioli are very susceptible to them, but only the small early ones are likely to be grown indoors. Keeping the air around the plants moist by misting will discourage thrips. If you are growing such bulbs on after flowering the plants can be inverted into a bucket of water with a little detergent or insecticide if thrips appear. Hold the compost in with a piece of cloth or paper.

Diseases are much more likely to cause difficulties. Sometimes bulbs are already infected when they are purchased, which is one reason why I like to be able to pick mine out myself, turning each over and examining it closely for dark discoloured spots and blotches before deciding to purchase it. By mail order I frequently get some diseased bulbs included with the good ones and if they are badly infected I pack them up and send them back immediately.

Those that are only slightly marked I dust with a fungicide such as quintozene, which is available in a dry formulation known as Botrilex, made expressly for this purpose. It may be necessary to remove the dry, loose outer coats from some bulbs and corms to make quite sure that they really are clean and healthy. When removing the mouldy skins from hyacinths you may find your skin irritates badly. Whether this is due to the fungus or something the bulb growers use I do not know. Wash in clear water and it will soon go.

Unfortunately there is no way of telling at this stage whether they are infected with any virus disease, since the symptoms only show up as the plants grow. Usually the leaves are mottled two shades of green or green and cream or white. They may also be rather distorted and the growth lacking in vigour. Though there are techniques for ridding some plants of virus infection they are not of a kind that can be applied at home. Since viruses can be spread rapidly from plant to plant, carried by greenflies, thrips or simply on one's fingers by touching the leaves, it is best to burn suspected plants as soon as they are detected. Some lilies are particularly susceptible to virus infection, but many kinds are seldom if ever attacked. Good growers take a lot of trouble to remove virus infected plants from their stocks, so the best safeguard is to buy only from firms of repute.

It is also almost always wise to buy the largest bulbs you can afford. The small grades may be cheaper, but they are unlikely to be anything like so satisfactory grown in containers. It is, as I have already stressed, the fat bulb that has most food reserves and also is most certain to flower—maybe even to produce several flowers. You may, however, prefer to have only one good spike from a hyacinth rather than one pushed over sideways by a second smaller and later one, and it will be found that the prepared hyacinths are often not quite as big as the unprepared, since the growers realize this and select accordingly.

This emphasis on size does not apply anything like so much to corms and tubers. Very small ones are to be avoided but often a middle size will perform just as well—some think even better—than a very big one so it is sensible to buy these and so save a little on price.

Section II. Recommended Kinds

Anemone
Some anemones make little gnarled tubers, and a few of these make good indoor plants in well drained pots or deep seed pans. All are by nature spring flowering, though indoors they may open earlier. For preference they should be grown in soil composts, such as JIP1, and can be planted from August to October.

Space the little tubers $1\frac{1}{2}$ inches apart and cover them $\frac{1}{2}$ inch deep. Start them in a cool place, outdoors if possible, and only bring them into a warm room when they are about to flower. Even then put them in bright diffuse light. If put into direct sunlight in a south facing window the flowers fade rapidly. They will need such a position after flowering to complete their growth, but if it is intended to put them outside to complete their growth they will need hardening off first. When all the leaves have died down the little tubers can be collected and stored in a cool dry place in bags with a little dry peat to prevent the buds being knocked off. Replant in autumn.

Water is needed all the time the plants are in leaf. From about February until the leaves start to die down a little liquid fertiliser can be added to the water every 10-14 days.

The best kind for indoor cultivation is *Anemone blanda* with blue, white, pink or carmine and white flowers on slender 2 to 3 inch stems. *A. coronaria* and *A. fulgens*, both with scarlet flowers on quite sturdy

8 to 12 inch stems, are very striking plants, but less easy to manage indoors because of their need for strong light. The same is true of the garden strains, such as De Caen and St. Brigid, the former with single flowers, the latter semi-double, in a good range of colours including shades of pink, red, blue and purple.

Fig. 1.
Anemone fulgens.

Babiana (Baboon root).
These are small South African plants grown from corms. There are several different kinds, mostly very attractive, but very few are offered commercially in Britain. Any obtainable should be potted in autumn, the earlier the better, in JIP1 with a little extra sand for quick drainage, in drained containers. If only to be retained indoors up to flowering they can be grown in half pots, but if it is intended to grow corms for the following year they must be in full depth pots as the new corms are formed quite deeply in the soil. Five to 7 corms are sufficient for a 5 inch pot; smaller diameter pots lack the necessary depth. Fed well they produce attractive, slightly hairy, pleated leaves, several to each corm.

Most babianas are nearly hardy and all require a good light position and plenty of water during their growing period. They are often better in a sunny verandah or a sunroom, provided it is frost proof, than indoors, though an unheated room can be used until they come into flower. The spikes of flowers may need some light staking in the taller varieties (up to 12 inches) though many will only be 6 to 8 inches high. The leaves turn brown shortly after flowering, when watering should cease, but the corms are best left in the pots in a sunny position until replanting, when they should be put in fresh compost and near the top again or the roots will go straight out of the drainage holes.

It is unusual today to be able to buy anything but mixed babianas.

This usually means colour forms of *Babiana stricta*, though occasionally there are some hybrid forms. The flowers, several on a stem, are blue, violet, cerise or almost white edged with bluish-violet. Yellow, and red-throated blue are rare.

Begonia.
Many kinds of begonia are fibrous rooted and so do not concern us here. The showy tuberous rooted varieties suitable for indoor cultivation are all hybrids and fall into three main groups, Large Flowered, Multiflora and Pendula. Of these the two last are to be preferred in rooms since the large flowered varieties are rather unwieldy and require careful support. Both multiflora and pendula types have smaller but more numerous flowers, the difference between them being that the multiflora have fairly stiff upward growing stems, making a bushy type of plant, whereas the stems of the pendula varieties are longer, more flexible and tend to hang down. They can be grown in suspended baskets or placed in a display stand and allowed to trail over the edge.

Tubers can be purchased in the spring. They should be started into growth by being half buried, close together in seed trays filled with moist peat and kept in a temperature of 18 to 20°C. When they have two or three small leaves each they are potted singly into 5 inch pots in JIP1 or

Fig. 2. A Large Flowered begonia 'Clarissa Hutchinson'.

peat potting compost, the tubers still kept well up, almost on the surface of the compost.

Indoors the best place for begonias is an east or west facing window, i.e. with good light but not too much sunshine. (In greenhouses begonias are lightly shaded in summer). It will help if the pots can be placed in display stands with damp peat or moss packed around them, for this will keep the air a little moist, which is what they like. They should be watered sufficiently to keep the compost moist right through, and in summer, as they come into flower, can be fed every 7 to 10 days with weak liquid fertiliser. In autumn they should be allowed to become dry gradually, so that the leaves die down. Then the tubers can be stored in bags in a dry, frost proof place (a cupboard will do provided it is not too warm) until it is time to start all over again the following spring.

These begonias are usually sold in separate colours: white, pink, red, crimson, orange and yellow, and also in mixture. Multiflora Maxima varieties have rather larger flowers than the ordinary Multiflora, mostly double, and may be preferred as pot plants.

Chionodoxa (Glory of the Snow).
Very pretty plants with short sprays of starry flowers in spring. They are grown from bulbs which should be planted in early autumn in pots or

Fig. 3. Chionodoxa luciliae, Glory of the Snow.

dwarf pots, about 7 bulbs in the 5 inch diameter or 9 or 10 in $5\frac{1}{2}$ to 6 inch size. Grow in either soil or soilless compost and keep in a cool place until the flower stems are well developed, when they can be brought into the living room for a week or so while they are in bloom. Keep out of hot sun, which will shorten their life, and remember that the warmer the room the shorter the flowering period. After flowering the leaves and the flower stems lengthen considerably and at this stage they are better outdoors, but they should be kept watered until they die down in early summer, after which they can be kept dry until September or just left in their pots to take such rain as may fall on them.

One of the best kinds is *Chionodoxa luciliae* with sky blue, white centred flowers. There is also a lilac pink form which I consider less attractive, especially indoors where colours tend to be paler. Other kinds are *C. gigantea* with larger flowers than *C. luciliae*, but not quite such bright, clear cut colouring, and *C. sardensis*, which is a deeper blue. It is also possible to obtain white forms of both *C. luciliae* and *C. gigantea*.

Crocus.
Everyone knows the large spring flowering crocuses with their very showy white, lavender, purple or yellow flowers. What many people do not realise is that there are a number of other kinds of crocus, some flowering a good deal earlier than these Dutch hybrid varieties, a few in mid-winter or even in autumn. All are smaller in flower than the Dutch hybrids, but they are often more shapely and they contain a lot of colours and colour combinations not found in the big flowers. All, large and small, hybrid and wild species alike, can be grown in containers, which should be drained and can be filled with either soil or soilless compost.

Crocuses grow from small corms and succeed well in fairly deep seed pans. A dwarf pot $5\frac{1}{2}$ to 6 inches in diameter will take 9 or 10 corms according to size and look very lovely for a few weeks, though once the flowers fade the leaves lengthen rapidly and cease to be decorative.

It is wise to start cool, in fact, since they are all perfectly hardy and a six months succession of bloom can be had simply by choosing varieties that flower naturally at different times, there is really nothing to be gained by using artificial heat at any time. The pots can stand outdoors until the flower buds begin to spear through the compost, or if there is no such convenient place, they can be kept in the coolest, lightest room in the house. While outside they must be protected from mice which eat them greedily. A simple precaution is to cover the pans with fine mesh wire netting, well pegged down.

The time to bring them into the living room or office is directly the flower buds are well formed, but before they begin to open, and even then the cooler the room the longer they will last in flower.

Keep the soil nicely moist until the leaves begin to wither, after which no further water is required. Liquid feeding is unlikely to be necessary.

After flowering they can go outside again or be tapped out carefully and planted in the garden, but so long as they are not forced unduly in heat and are well looked after crocuses can be grown year after year in containers. If this is the plan they should be taken out of the pots in July, graded according to size and only the best repotted in fresh compost. The small ones should either be discarded or planted out in some place where it does not matter much if they miss one year's flowering.

Dutch crocuses are available in mixtures of all colours, in separate colours or as 'named' varieties which have been selected and propagated for their excellence. Good varieties are 'Enchantress', pale blue; 'Jeanne d'Arc', white; 'Pickwick', white feathered with purple; 'Purpureus Grandiflorus', purple; 'Striped Beauty', white striped with purple; and 'Yellow Giant', yellow.

The following are good species or varieties of species:

Crocus ancyrensis. Small but intensely bright orange yellow flowers very freely produced in January.

C. chrysanthus. Small but beautifully formed flowers, freely produced in February. This kind is very variable in colour and the following are good named varieties. 'Blue Bird', purplish blue and white; 'Blue Pearl',

Fig. 4. Crocus chrysanthus.

light blue; 'Cream Beauty', cream; 'E.A. Bowles', deep yellow feathered outside with bronze; 'Ladykiller', two shades, bluish purple with white edges; 'Snowbunting', white feathered with bronze, bright orange stigmas; 'Zwanenburg', bright yellow inside, but heavily marked with bronze outside.
C. imperatii. Flowers buff outside, lavender blue inside, opening in January.
C. tomasinianus. The wild form is rather a pale lilac, but there are richer coloured varieties such as 'Taplow Ruby', reddish purple, and 'Whitewell Purple', violet purple. All flower in January or February.
C. sieberi. Mauve flowers which are feathered with purple in 'Hubert Edelsten'; opening in February.
C. speciosus. Lavender blue, or white in 'Albus'; both flowering in September or October.
C. susianus. Called "Cloth of Gold" which well describes its brilliant golden yellow colour. Flowers in February, March.
C. zonatus (kotschyanus). Lilac pink flowers in September.

Cyclamen.
The foliage of some varieties of cyclamen is as decorative as their flowers and since it is there for about nine months of the year it considerably enhances their value as indoor plants. The varieties commonly sold for this purpose are all highly developed forms of *Cyclamen persicum* with flowers very much larger than those of the wild plant from which they have been developed, and with a colour range from white and palest pink to scarlet and crimson. Usually, however, these giant garden forms lack the sweet scent of the wild plant and the flowers are less dainty and butter-fly-like. Smaller flowered varieties have also been selected, one strain of these being marketed as 'Puck'. These are less spectacular, but very attractive and just the thing for a narrow window ledge.

There are also numerous other kinds of cyclamen, all smaller than *C. persicum*, and some completely hardy and commonly grown out of doors, though they can be grown perfectly well in drained containers such as flower pots, dwarf pots and deep seed pans. Though not so spectacular as the big Persian cyclamen some of these hardy kinds are extremely attractive and they flower at different times of the year.

All cyclamen are increased by seed, but seed germinates rather slowly and irregularly, and it takes about a year for seedlings to reach flowering size so most people prefer to start with flowering plants or dry tubers. The latter are normally only available for hardy varieties and are not very satisfactory if they have been kept for a long time out of the ground, since cyclamen only have a short resting season and even then do not like to be quite dry. Also the buds on some tubers are borne on little protuberances which are easily knocked off. As the tubers do not readily make more, these tubers are then useless. It is best to keep dormant tubers in soil always and to buy growing plants in pots.

However, if dry tubers are purchased, they should be placed shoulder to shoulder in seed trays filled with moist peat. Just bed them in the peat, rounded side downwards, without covering them completely and without rubbing off the small buds on top, and keep them moist until they begin to produce leaves. Then pot them singly in either JIP1 or soilless potting compost, keeping the tubers practically on the surface. The roots grow from the bottom of the tuber and the leaves and flowers from the almost flat, or even slightly concave, upper surface. The tubers get wider and wider with age, never splitting up or producing new ones as bulbs and corms do. In time the tubers can get so big that it is quite difficult to repot them and professional gardeners usually discard the greenhouse varieties after flowering, preferring to rely on new seedlings for the best results. However there is no need to do this and I have tubers that are many years old and still growing and flowering well.

Cyclamen persicum and its varieties flower in winter and early spring and rest for a few weeks in summer. Most other varieties follow a similar pattern, the resting time varying with the flowering time.

In containers the routine is to keep the plants well watered throughout

Fig. 5. Cyclamen persicum.

the period during which they are growing and flowering, but to keep the soil only just moist when the foliage turns yellow and dies down. At this stage it is an advantage if the containers can be placed outdoors in the shade.

Then, after six or eight weeks, new leaves will start to appear in a ring on the top of the tuber, and this is the time to repot and to start heavier watering again. Large flowered cyclamen should be repotted annually either in JIP2 for established plants (JIP1 for seedlings or newly started tubers) or in a soilless compost, most of the old compost being shaken off. Cyclamen species do not take kindly to such drastic disturbance and it is sufficient to remove a little of the lower soil and replace with fresh. I think they succeed best in soil composts. In either soil or soilless compost the large flowered varieties should be fed with weak liquid fertiliser every 10 to 14 days from the time the leaves are well developed until they start to turn yellow. Cyclamen species seldom need extra feeding.

Anyone wishing to raise cyclamen from seed should sow in August in a seed compost. Cover the seed pan with a sheet of glass and a piece of paper, but remove both when the first seedlings appear. Lift these carefully and pot them singly in JIP1 in $2\frac{1}{2}$ inch pots when they have two or three leaves, but do not discard the seed pan as more seedlings may appear later (sometimes as much as a year later).

The first year from seed cyclamen do not rest at all, but go on growing winter and summer. They will need to be moved on to larger pots as they fill the smaller ones with roots—first into 3 or $3\frac{1}{2}$ inch pots, then to the 4 or 5 inch pots in which they will flower. Few plants like being in pots very much too large for them.

C. persicum and its varieties are rather tender and should not be exposed to frost at any time, but neither do they like hot, dry rooms. A temperature of 15 to 20°C is ample and from September to May they like all the light that is going. A window ledge is the best place for them or better still a sun lounge or glazed verandah, provided it is frost proof at night.

The large flowered varieties derived from *Cyclamen persicum* are sold in mixed colours, but there are several different strains, some with particularly heavily silvered leaves.

Cyclamen species which may be grown in pots or pans are:

Cyclamen coum. Small pink or carmine flowers on 3 inch stems from November to March. Dark green or mottled kidney shaped leaves, sometimes red beneath.

C. europaeum. Fragrant pink or carmine flowers on 3 inch stems in late summer. Kidney shaped leaves, sometimes mottled, dark red beneath. Evergreen.

C. libanoticum. Pink flowers on 6 to 8 inch stems in February, March. Slightly scented and changing colour from pale to deep pink as it ages. Unlike most cyclamen the petals do not twist. Leaves dark green with paler green markings. Needs to be dormant in a sunny place and is not fully hardy.

C. hederaefolium (neopolitan) Flowers pink (or white in variety Album) on 4 inch stems from August to October. Ivy shaped leaves mottled with silver or light green. Roots only from the upper surface of the tuber.

C. persicum. Pink or white flowers on 6 to 9 inch stems in spring. Sweetly scented. Variable foliage, often handsomely mottled with silver.

C. repandum. Pink, crimson or white flowers on 6 to 8 inch stems in spring. Ivy shaped leaves mottled with silver.

Eranthis (Winter Aconite).
These are one of the first flowers to open in January out of doors, and they will come even earlier in the warm temperature of a living room. They are grown from little tubers which can be planted 8 to 10 together in a $5\frac{1}{2}$ or 6 inch half pot in either JIP1 or peat potting compost. September is the time to pot and the tubers should be covered about $\frac{3}{4}$ inch deep. The cooler they can be kept for the first month or so the better, but as soon as they are rooting well they can come into ordinary room temperature which will quickly bring them into flower. The flowers on 2 to 3 inch stems are yellow, rather like buttercups, but with a green ruff of bracts below each bloom. The leaves come a little later and are much divided, which makes them a very attractive carpeting plant outside. By this stage they are happier in the cooler, moister atmosphere outside than in a room. If there is a place for them in a shady bed or under deciduous shrubs they can be put out permanently.

The two best kinds are *Eranthis hyemalis* and *E. tubergenii*, the latter a hybrid with larger flowers and longer stems.

Fig. 6.
One of the winter flowering aconites, Eranthis tubergeniana.

Freesia.
The easiest way to grow freesias is to buy corms in August or September and pot them at once 1 inch deep, with 6 or 7 in each 5 inch pot of JIP1 or soilless compost. A cheaper method, but one involving a good deal more time and care, is to buy seed and sow it in February or March very thinly in similar compost and pots. In ordinary room temperature the seeds will germinate in a fortnight or so and thereafter the seedlings are kept growing undisturbed until they have flowered. They should not be transplanted. When the leaves have died down the corms can be shaken out and stored till late summer. From June to September the plants can be stood outdoors in a sunny place, but they must never be exposed to frost. Keep a sharp look out for greenflies outdoors.

Seedlings will usually start to flower about November, whereas corms potted in September are unlikely to start flowering until February, or even March, if grown cool, so the two methods of cultivation do ensure a longer succession of bloom.

Freesias come from South Africa and like so many plants from that country they enjoy sunshine, so a south facing window is the place for them, if they cannot be started in a frostproof greenhouse. They are nearly, but not quite, hardy so high temperatures are not necessary. The flower stems are thin and though wiry need support from an early stage. This is best given by pushing three or four small sticks into the compost around the edge of each pot and encircling these with several strands of fillis. In poor light the stems can get very long and twisted, which is another reason for giving them the sunniest place.

When the foliage eventually dies down in spring or early summer the corms can either be shaken out and stored in bags in a cool dry place until it is time to repot them and start all over again, or left in their pots, without water, if this is more convenient. In any case they should be replanted into fresh soil, and the best of the corms, which will be found several inches down, should be replanted near the top. They increase rapidly, and you should get two pots from each old one.

Colours available include shades of yellow, orange, blue and red, plus white. All the modern strains are deliciously fragrant, though some of the first coloured strains had little scent. One pot of freesias is sufficient to scent quite a large room. There are also double flowered varieties available which have much stronger stems.

Galanthus (Snowdrop).
There are numerous different kinds of snowdrop and all can be grown successfully in drained containers in either soil or soilless compost, though I prefer the former. JIP1 will keep them going for a full year without any extra feeding, and in this kind of compost the bulbs can be used again and

again without the chance of becoming exhausted.

Dwarf pots make excellent containers for snowdrops and a 5½ or 6 inch diameter pot will easily take 10 to 12 bulbs.

Snowdrops do not like being out of the ground for long, so buy the bulbs as early in September as you can and pot them at once, covering them ½ inch deep. They enjoy cool conditions at all times, so do not bring them into a heated room until they are about to flower; early heat appears to slow up flower production. Until about to flower they can be kept anywhere outdoors—on a window ledge or balcony, in the garden or in any other convenient place, in sun or shade. If there is no place for them outside keep them in an unheated room, garage or shed. They do not need light until coming through the soil, when they need the lightest place possible, especially those kinds which come from the eastern Mediterranean areas. Most snowdrops push their flowers up slightly ahead of the two surrounding leaves, so it is possible to have them in the warm as soon as they show signs of growth above soil level. The leaves eventually grow very long, as do the flower stems, and at this stage look very untidy, though the wide leaved species are not quite so bad as *G. nivalis*.

Water moderately at all times, and even in early summer do not let the

Fig. 7. One of the snowdrop species, Galanthus ikariae.

compost get quite dry, as it is at this time that next years flowers are being formed inside the bulbs. The best time to plant out into the garden is immediately after flowering, but the plants can be kept in the pots outside until September, if this is more convenient. But then they should be repotted before the bulbs start to make fresh roots. There will probably be many more bulbs than originally planted and these can be put into other pots or graded, keeping the largest for potting, and growing the others elsewhere.

The following are good kinds, all flowering in January or February:
Galanthus elwesii. This has extra large flowers on 7 inch stems and broad leaves. It is often obtainable imported direct from Greece and Turkey and these bulbs are sometimes difficult to get started into growth, possibly needing a period of cold first. The snowdrop named 'Colesbourne' is very similar.
G. ikariae. This has large flowers, rather short stems and broad leaves which are not glaucous as in many snowdrops, but bright green.
G. nivalis. The common snowdrop, native to Britain and better able to cope with semi-shade than the other species. It is a charming plant which has produced numerous varieties. Specially recommended are *flore pleno*, the double flowered snowdrop, very distinctive and free flowering; 'Atkinsii', flowers larger and stems longer than the wild form; 'S. Arnott' (sometimes called Arnott's Seedling), much like 'Atkinsii'.
G. plicatus. The largest flowered of all with quite long stems and broad leaves.

Gladiolus.

The showy summer-flowering gladioli need no introduction, but they are too tall and too short lived in flower to make satisfactory pot plants. Far better for this purpose are the smaller spring and early summer flowering hybrids sold as *Gladiolus nanus* or *G. colvillei*.

All gladioli are grown from corms. Those of the big summer-flowering kinds are planted in spring and are stored dry from October until March or even later, but the early flowering kinds grow all winter, rest in July and August and are potted in September or October.

Plant 6 or 7 corms in a $5\frac{1}{2}$ or 6 inch pot in JIP1 compost. Keep in a light, cool but frost proof place (a window ledge in an unheated room will do well except in the coldest weather), water sparingly at first, but more freely as the leaves lengthen.

Feed every 10 to 14 days from mid-April to mid-June, but after flowering reduce the water supply and let the soil become virtually dry. At this period the pots can stand outdoors in a sunny place as any rain that falls on them will do no harm. Repot in September, but only the well developed corms, as very small ones are unlikely to flower the next year.

Recommended varieties of *Gladiolus nanus* (syn. *colvillei*) are 'Amanda

May', salmon pink; 'Blushing Bride', white flecked with pink; 'Charm', lilac; 'Peach Blossom', pink and cream; 'Spitfire', scarlet; and 'The Bride', white.

Corms are occasionally available of *G. tristis*, a species with rush-like leaves and small, pale sulphur yellow, sweetly scented flowers in April-May.

Haemanthus.

These curious bulbs produce their broad, fleshy leaves in pairs, pressed together at the base and folded outwards in opposite directions like the pages of an open book. The stout flower stem comes up between the leaves and terminates in a more or less globular cluster of tubular flowers with long protruding stamens making the whole thing look rather like a coloured brush. They are not difficult to grow, but to get them to flower well they must have plenty of sun and warmth in summer—which indoors means that they must have a sunny window ledge most of the time. They should be obtained in summer or early autumn and be grown in drained containers, preferably pots, in JIP1 compost. Though it is often said that they should be given large pots, my experience is that they do well in pots just large enough to take the bulbs comfortably, which may be anything from 4 inch for a young bulb of a fairly small kind, such as white flowered *Haemanthus albiflos*, to 7 inch for an old bulb of a larger kind, such as scarlet flowered *H. katherinae*.

All flower in winter or spring and die down in summer, at which time they should be kept dry but should not be disturbed. Repotting is only likely to be necessary every second or third year and in the meantime the plants can be fed every 14 days or so in spring with a little liquid fertiliser added to the water.

Hippeastrum.

This is the correct name for bulbs that are often marketed as amaryllis, a different plant less suitable for indoor cultivation. Hippeastrums have immensely showy trumpet-shaped flowers, usually produced four together on a sturdy bare stem. The common colour is bright red, but there are also white, pink and white, pink and crimson varieties.

Bulbs specially prepared for early flowering are available in autumn and for this first flowering they are about as fool proof as anything one can buy. All that is necessary is to pot them and bring them straightaway into ordinary room temperature. In a few days they will start to grow and a few weeks later will be in bloom. The difficulties arise in ensuring repeat performances each year.

Some may settle for repurchase of bulbs each autumn, but they are fairly expensive and there is extra satisfaction in growing one's own. Another merit is that home grown bulbs do not all flower at the same time, but spread over several months in spring and summer.

For permanency hippeastrums should be grown in drained pots, preferably in JIP2 compost. They should be potted so that only the lower half of the large bulb is buried, the rest being exposed to light and air. Throughout the year they should be given all the light possible to keep the leaves growing well, since it is possible to get a flower stem after every fourth leaf (once the bulb has reached flowering size). Hippeastrums are not periodic flowerers, like the spring bulbs, nor are they dependent on any special day length to trigger off their flower formation, but they do need the light to help build up the necessary food, made as a result of photosynthesis. Because of this high light requirement it is easier to manage hippeastrums in a greenhouse, sun-room or glazed verandah, but they can be grown successfully in a sunny room, placed as close as possible to the window, except when this might expose them to frost.

In their natural habitats the hippeastrums have no dormant period, and the giant hybrids are also in leaf all the year if kept moist, losing and replacing a leaf at a time. Commercial growers wish to sell the bulbs in a dry state, however, and thus stop watering them in summer or early autumn, which gives dry bulbs which can be marketed from autumn onwards. Many gardeners do much the same, though probably most continue watering until September or October. Often they believe that this is essential, which it is not, the main advantage being that, if treated in this manner, new leaves appear shortly after the flower stem has started into growth and are still quite short when the flowers open. This gives a more pleasing, neater-looking plant than one grown naturally, which will have many old leaves and a few new ones. I know of no evidence that one method produces more regular flowering than the other. I do think that sunshine and occasional feeding in spring and summer, while plants are growing rapidly, helps to produce enough food to bring the young flower buds to maturity. A little liquid fertiliser can be added to the water every 10 to 14 days. Given this treatment most bulbs will flower annually, many producing a second flower spike about a month after the first.

Well fed bulbs produce small bulbs at the side (offsets), and if it is proposed to grow these on they must be removed just before the mother bulb is dried off. Remove the plant from its pot and shake off any loose soil. Frequently it will be found that the roots of bulb and offset are inextricably mixed. It is essential to keep the roots of the offsets intact, and if necessary the soil compost can be washed off so that the roots are more clearly seen. If any have to be broken it should be those of the bulb to be dried. The roots of hippeastrums are branched, unlike those of many bulbs, but even so they do not recover from damage in the same way as those of a tomato plant, for instance. Repot the offsets singly and keep them growing, with no drying off, but adequate moisture and feeding. They will not send up any flower stem until after they have produced nine good leaves, and only then if they have made a good bulb with plenty of reserve food. During the summer they produce a leaf about once a month, less frequently in dull winter weather.

Hyacinthus (Hyacinth).
These are easy bulbs to grow but not by any means the cheapest to buy. Two quite distinct types are available, the ordinary hyacinths which produce one massive spike of bloom per bulb, and the Roman hyacinths, also known as Multiflora hyacinths, which have several more slender flower spikes per bulb, with smaller, more loosely arranged flowers. The large flowered type is the most popular and offers the greatest selection of varieties, but Roman hyacinths grow very fast and look most attractive planted several

*Fig. 8.
An early
flowering
hyacinth.*

together in bowls or dwarf pots. Both types are richly scented.

Hyacinth bulbs are also available as lifted in the natural condition, or as 'prepared' bulbs, which means that after being lifted from the field they have been given carefully controlled heat treatment to hasten the initiation of flower buds and prepare the bulbs for early flowering. Either type of bulb should be given cool treatment before being brought into the warm, since hyacinths have a cold requirement (see Chapter 4) without which they will not grow and flower normally. Since it is difficult to give this cool treatment naturally until October there is no point in potting hyacinths before the last week in September. In order to obtain a succession of bloom some bulbs can be held back for late October or even November potting, but these should be ordinary bulbs. The 'prepared' bulbs should be planted in late September or early October.

Hyacinths will flower well in undrained bowls filled with special bulb fibre. For this method place the bulbs almost shoulder to shoulder in the bowls and leave the tops of the bulbs showing. Bowls can be flooded by rain water if placed outside, so after watering well they should be wrapped in moist newspaper to help keep the temperature down and put in the coolest place indoors. The temperature to aim at is 9°C or less, and this is needed for at least 8 weeks for prepared bulbs and 12 for ordinary ones. Darkness is an advantage at this stage so a cellar or cool cupboard is a suitable place.

Still better results can be obtained by growing hyacinths in drained containers. It is just possible to get one small bulb into a 4 inch pot, but a better effect is produced by growing 3 bulbs in a 6 inch pot. Use either a soil compost such as JIP1 or a soilless compost and leave the tips of the bulbs exposed. Give a period of cold treatment as described for hyacinths in undrained containers, but in drained containers this can be out of doors, preferably with the pots covered with 3 or 4 inches of moist peat, leafmould or washed sand, all of which should be kept moist to allow evaporation to occur and thus lower the temperature. It also keeps the bulbs in the dark.

From the time of planting until the leaves begin to turn yellow the soil or compost needs to be kept nicely moist. During the period when the flower stem is rapidly elongating water is used very quickly, so more must be given. From the stage when the flower spikes have emerged but the flower stem has not yet elongated a little fertiliser can be added to the water every 10 to 14 days. Over-watering in winter can cause the whole flower spike to become detached from the bulb, and so can the use of ammonium sulphate in fertiliser if applied in the autumn.

The best time to bring the hyacinths into a warm room is when the flower spikes have emerged from the bulb but before the stems have become visible. Place in a good light, as on a window sill, and turn the container through a quarter circle daily so that the stems do not grow towards the source of light. Indoors it is often necessary to stake the flower stems of hyacinths, and this should be done early before the weight of the heavy bloom pulls the bulb from its shallow bowl. Better than staking each stem separately is three split canes around the edge of a pot, and restraining strands of soft fillis. There is usually difficulty in staking in bowls, with curved, shallow bases, and in these the supports will be better nearer the centre, with loops of fillis outwards. Occasionally flower stems twist however good the light or early the staking, and this has been proved to be due to treatment of the bulbs designed to make them flower early.

After flowering the drained pots can go outside but not the undrained bowls because of the danger of waterlogging. These must be kept in some place where their rather unsightly appearance does not matter, or by mid-April the bulbs can be carefully tipped out with roots and fibre intact and planted outdoors.

It is best to start afresh with new bulbs each autumn, either discarding the old or planting them outdoors. Nevertheless, despite what the experts say, it is possible sometimes to flower hyacinths several years running in containers if they are well managed. For one thing they do not usually split up into a mass of small, non-flowering size bulbs but produce one big bulb and at most a few small off-sets. By mid-June all the leaves are likely to have died down and then the bulbs can be lifted, the best put aside for replanting in the autumn. Any small ones can either be discarded or planted in some place where it does not matter if they fail to flower the following year. A dusting of bone meal before planting will help them to grow well.

If bulb glasses are used instead of containers fill each with rain water just to the ledge on which the bulb will rest and drop a small lump of charcoal into each glass to keep the water sweet. Then place the bulb on its ledge and stand the glasses in a cool dark place. It will be easy to see how the roots are progressing and when they have filled much of the glass it is time to bring the plants into the light. Again it is a sunny window that will suit them best, and they too will need turning to keep the flower stems straight. Discard after flowering as they are not suitable for using the following year.

Roman hyacinths are available in white, pale blue and pink varieties, and the Multiflora hyacinths, which are not readily distinguishable from them, in these colours and red, yellow and deep blue also, for they are obtained by special treatment of the normal large stemmed type, except in 'Borah', which normally gives several stems without any treatment, (it is blue).

Good varieties of the large flowered hyacinths are 'L'Innocence', early white; 'Carnegie', late white; 'City of Haarlem', pale yellow; 'Anna Marie' (Ann Mary), bright pink; 'Lady Derby', pale pink; 'Pink Pearl', light carmine, early forcer: 'Jan Bos', crimson, forces well; 'La Victoire', carmine; 'Bismark', light blue; 'Delft Blue', pale blue; 'King of the Blues', indigo blue; 'Ostara', dark blue, forces well; and 'Chestnut Flower', a fine late double flowered variety.

Iris.
The irises to grow in containers are the very early bulbous rooted kinds. They do well in dwarf pots in exactly the same conditions as crocuses. Like them, the narrow leaves, short, stiffly erect and quite attractive when the flowers open, quickly lengthen after that and flop about untidily, so

these are another example of bulbs that should not be kept on show all the time, but should be brought in for the week or two while they are in bloom and be kept in some fairly inconspicuous place at other times. They can be grown for several years in pots if well cared for, but *Iris danfordiae* can be difficult as the flowering bulbs tend to split up into numerous small ones, none of which is sufficiently large to flower again for several years. The surest way of getting a display is to buy new bulbs each autumn—the earlier the better as they really need to be potted in September.

Grow in JIP1 or soilless compost, the former being better if it is intended to grow the bulbs on for a second year. Place about 7 bulbs in a $5\frac{1}{2}$ or 6 inch dwarf pot, covering them to a depth of about $\frac{1}{2}$ inch. Give them at least 10 weeks cold treatment, preferably outdoors in a plunge bed of damp peat or sand, but failing this in a cellar, garage or other cold place. Better as a guide than a rule of thumb number of weeks is to watch for the first emergence of shoots, a signal that the bulbs are well rooted, will soon flower and can safely be brought indoors, but preferably to an unheated room as iris flowers are short lived even in the most favourable conditions and may last no more than three or four days in a warm room. After flowering stand outdoors, if possible. Keep the compost moist until late May, then let the foliage die down naturally. If the old bulbs are kept for growing a second time, repot in fresh compost in August or early September and only use the best bulbs. The rest can be planted outdoors in well drained soil and a sunny place. Protect them against mice and voles.
The following are recommended kinds:

Iris danfordiae. Yellow flowers on 4 inch stems in January or early February. Easy to grow and flower the first year, but not so easy to keep flowering in subsequent years.

I. histrioides. The first to flower, often opening by Christmas indoors. The flowers are sturdy and carried on 3 inch stems. The variety usually offered is 'Major', which is light blue with yellow markings, but there are also deeper blue forms. This is an easy iris to grow and one that usually multiplies readily and goes on flowering year after year.

I. reticulata. This is the most variable in colour of all the small early flowering species. The flowers are more slender than those of *I. histrioides*, are carried on longer, 6 inch stems, and open a few weeks later in February. They are always violet scented. The typical colour is violet purple splashed with gold, but 'Cantab' is light blue, and 'Krelagei' is plum purple.

Ixia.

Because these South African plants like plenty of sunshine and make much of their growth in winter when that is not a conspicuous characteristic of the British climate, they cannot be regarded as ideal indoor plants. Yet they are so gay and different that they are worth trying if they can be

*Fig. 9.
A mixed collection
of ixias.*

given a south facing window, or, better still, a sun-room or glazed verandah. Provided the light is adequate and they do not get frozen there are no difficulties in growing them and they multiply rapidly.

The corms are small and up to a dozen can be accommodated in a 5 inch pot. They will grow readily in JIP1 or soilless compost and should be covered about $\frac{1}{2}$ inch. September is the best time to start and they can be brought indoors straightaway, or overwintered in any sunny, frost-proof structure such as a slightly heated greenhouse. The compost must be kept moist from potting time until the foliage starts to die down in summer. The long and narrow, rather grass-like leaves are not unattractive, so there is no need to hurry them out of the house after flowering, but from late May until October they can stand outdoors if desired. They should be shaken out and repotted in fresh compost each September.

Most of the corms offered are hybrids, with starry flowers carried in arching sprays on slender but wiry stems, which may be as much as 2 feet high. Mixed colours are usually offered, the range including carmine, scarlet, purple, blue, orange, yellow and white. The only species likely to be available is *Ixia viridiflora*, an unusual and beautiful plant with slender erect spikes of blue-green flowers, each with a nearly black centre. It is no more difficult to grow than the others, but a good deal harder to buy.

Lachenalia.
Charming South African plants with tubular flowers hanging in short spikes on bare stems in spring. They are not quite hardy enough to be grown outdoors except in a few very mild and sheltered places, but neither

do they like great heat, and so are best kept out of warm rooms until they are about to come into flower.

The bulbs should be grown in well drained containers, pots or dwarf pots being ideal. They should be potted as early as possible, in August if bulbs can be obtained then and certainly not later than September. A 5 inch pot will take about 5 bulbs. Use either JIP2 or a soilless potting compost and cover the bulbs to a depth of half an inch. Water rather sparingly at first as the young shoots may rot if too wet, but when the leaves are an inch or so long water fairly freely and continue to do so until the leaves start to die down after flowering. Feed with very weak liquid fertiliser every 10 to 14 days from about February to May.

Throughout most of the growing season a temperature range of 13° to 18°C is ideal. Most living rooms are warmer than this, but a sunny window in an unheated room or a sun-room or glazed verandah will suit them well. If they must be in a living room or office put them near the window but not near a radiator or other heat source. After flowering lachenalias enjoy all the sun and warmth they can get to ripen the bulbs.

Lachenalias cannot safely be planted outdoors, but they can be pot grown year after year, and should be repotted annually in August. Shake the bulbs completely free of the old compost and start them afresh in new compost.

Fig. 10.
The spring snowflake,
Leucojum vernum.

The best kinds are:
Lachenalia aloides, also known as *L. tricolor*, a good descriptive name since the tubular flowers are in three colours, yellow, red and green.
L. bulbifera. Coral red, yellow tipped flowers, held outwards rather than completely pendulous as in *L. aloides*.
L. nelsonii. Similar to *L. aloides*, of which it is usually regarded as a variety, but the flowers are yellow and green without any red.

Leucojum. (Snowflake).
The best snowflake for growing indoors is *Leucojum vernum*. This looks like a rather big snowdrop, though the flowers are much more bell-shaped. They flower, like snowdrops, in February and are carried on 6 to 8 inch stems. Cultivation is exactly the same as for snowdrops (*Galanthus*, p.23).

Lilium (Lily).
It would be difficult to manage any lilies indoors on a long term basis, but it is possible to obtain bulbs of some varieties specially prepared for rapid growth and flowering. These need not be potted until December and in ordinary room temperature, without any preliminary cold treatment, will then flower in from eight to twelve weeks, after which they can go outside to complete their growth. They cannot be made to repeat this

Fig. 11.
Lilium
'Enchantment',
one of the
Mid-Century
Hybrids.

lightning performance again the following year, but if reasonably lime free ground is available they can be planted outdoors, and if conditions are congenial may continue to thrive and multiply for years. As a rule it is the hybrid lilies with clusters of upward facing flowers, e.g. the Mid-Century Hybrids and others of like breeding, that are prepared for early flowering. Colours are mostly in shades of yellow, orange and red.

Muscari (Grape Hyacinth).
The small flowers of most kinds of grape hyacinth are packed tightly in little spikes only a few inches high. However there is one kind that is spectacularly different. This is *Muscari comosum monstrosum*, known as the feather hyacinth because the quite large flower spikes appear to be composed of innumerable blue filaments. Nor do the stems stand erect as in other kinds, but flop about under the weight of their bloom. Other good kinds, conventional in habit, are 'Heavenly Blue', a good form of *Muscari armeniacum*, with sky blue flowers; *M. botryoides*, much like the last, and with a good white form; and *M. tubergenianum*, a little beauty with flowers that are dark violet blue at the top of the spike and light blue at the bottom. All kinds can be grown in the same way as chionodoxa. (see p. 16-17).

Narcissus (Daffodil).
The two names are synonymous, one botanical, the other popular. There are a great many varieties grouped in various classes according to the character of the flower, e.g. trumpet daffodils with a long trumpet-like tube or corona, backed by a shorter circle of petals, the perianth; large cupped in which the corona is shorter than the perianth segments; small cupped, even shorter; tazetta and poetaz, both with a cluster of small flowers on each stem; double flowered, with numerous petals making a rounded, gardenia-like flower; poeticus, with a small yellow and red eye in the centre of a flat white perianth, and several more.

For retail sale narcissus bulbs are graded according to the number of flowers they should produce. Rounds are the cheapest and should have one embryo flower in each bulb. Double-nosed cost more, but have two embryo flowers and mother bulbs, rarely available, may produce three flowers each.

The bulbs do not have a long resting season and if they can be potted in August that is ideal. Usually, however, they are not available until about mid-September because of the time it takes to lift, clean, grade and dispatch. This is quite satisfactory, but the bulbs should be potted as soon as possible and not be kept in the bags for weeks. Bulbs specially prepared for early flowering are available of some varieties.

Narcissi can be grown in bulb fibre in undrained bowls, but they are not as satisfactory for this method of cultivation as hyacinths. They succeed best in flower pots of other fairly deep containers with proper drainage holes, filled with a good potting compost, either of the JIP2 type or a soilless mix.

Daffodil bulbs should be spaced so that they just do not touch and be put sufficiently low in the container so that the bulb is under the compost, but the dry tops of the scale leaves are visible, and yet there is a ½ inch space between the top of the compost and the rim of the container, for ease of watering.

Miniature daffodils, such as the cyclamen flowered daffodil (*Narcissus cyclamineus*), the hoop petticoat daffodil (*N. bulbocodium*) and the angel's-tears daffodil (*N. triandrus albus*) look delightful in dwarf pots and one 5½ or 6 inches in diameter will take eight to ten bulbs.

Most daffodils need at least 12 weeks in a cool place to make roots and prepare for flowering before they are brought into a warm room, but they are not so liable as hyacinths to make premature growth and then collapse. The exceptions to the cold treatment are the two very early forcing varieties, 'Scilly White' or (Paper White) and 'Grand Soleil d'Or', which can be brought into a warm place as soon as they have been planted. They can then be had in flower in from 6 to 10 weeks, 'Scilly White' usually being in flower in November.

Cold treatment for bulbs in drained containers is best given by covering

Fig. 12.
A fine potful of large cupped narcissus.

the pots with damp peat or sand at least 2 inches deep. In the shade of a north wall is ideal, but any out of the way place can be utilized. Leave them under the peat until the leaves begin to push through it, when the covering can be removed to rim level, but the pots should not be brought into the warm until the leaves are several inches high. If the weather is very cold and growth is completely checked it is possible to compromise by bringing them into a cold room, provided they can be in the light. If kept in a room from the start they can be put in a cold cupboard until the leaves are 2 inches high, after which light is essential.

Narcissi are fairly thirsty plants and the compost must never be allowed to become dry until the leaves are actually beginning to turn yellow. They are also fairly hungry plants and unless in a rich compost will benefit from feeding every 10 to 14 days with weak liquid fertilizer from the time the flower buds show until the leaves begin to yellow.

After flowering the foliage lengthens rapidly and the plants can become untidy. If space is available they can be planted straightaway outdoors as they are nearly all completely hardy (the chief exceptions are the very early tazetta varieties such as 'Grand Soleil d'Or' and 'Scilly White'), or alternatively they can be placed anywhere outdoors in sun or shade to complete their growth. It is not really desirable to keep on growing them in pots year after year, as even with the best of care they do slowly de-

Fig. 13. The hoop petticoat daffodil, Narcissus bulbocodium.

teriorate, but if there is no other place for them it is certainly worth using the best bulbs a second time.

Varieties are legion and all can be grown successfully. Here is a limited selection of varieties that I have grown and liked, but there are many more. They are grouped according to the classes in which they will be found in catalogues.

TRUMPET DAFFODILS. 'Dutch Master', yellow; 'Golden Harvest', yellow; 'Kingscourt', yellow; 'Louise de Coligny', apricot pink and white; 'Mount Hood', white; 'Rembrandt', yellow; 'Spellbinder', primrose and lime yellow; 'Trousseau', white and primrose; 'Unsurpassable', yellow.

LARGE-CUPPED. 'Binkie', sulphur and ivory white; 'Carlton', yellow; 'Eddy Canzony', white and orange; 'Fortune', yellow and orange; 'Ice Follies', white; 'Salmon Trout', white and salmon pink.

SMALL-CUPPED. 'Barrett Browning', white and orange-red; 'Birma', yellow and orange-red; 'Edward Buxton', yellow and orange; 'Verger', white and orange-red.

DOUBLE. 'Golden Ducat', yellow; 'Mary Copeland', white and orange-red; 'Texas', cream and orange-red; 'White Lion', white. These are all rather tall, but very showy.

CYCLAMINEUS HYBRIDS. 'February Gold', yellow; 'Peeping Tom', yellow.

TRIANDRUS HYBRIDS (small flowers in clusters). 'Silver Chimes', white; 'Thalia', white.

TAZETTA HYBRIDS AND POETAZ (cluster flowered). 'Cragford', white and orange; 'Geranium', white and orange-red; 'Laurens Koster', white and yellow; 'Scilly White', white; 'Soleil d'Or', yellow and orange.

POETICUS. 'Actaea', white with red and yellow eye.

SPECIES (all very small). *Narcissus bulbocodium conspicuus*, yellow, crinoline-shaped trumpet; *canaliculatus*, white and yellow, multiflowered; *cyclamineus*, narrow yellow trumpet, reflexed perianth segments; *jonquilla*, small, deep yellow, highly scented, multiflowered; *juncifolius*, small, light yellow, short cupped, multiflowered, highly scented; *triandrus albus*, clusters of small nodding white flowers.

Nerine (Diamond Lily, Guernsey Lily).
There are almost as many theories about the cultivation of these beautiful South African bulbs as there are growers. The reason for this diversity of opinion is not that they are in the least difficult to grow, but that some are extremely unpredictable in flower production. Some experts recommend a starvation diet, some good feeding, some want to dry and almost bake the bulbs in summer, some think it better not to dry them out completely at any time. Part of this diversity of opinion is undoubtedly due to the fact that many of the nerines grown in gardens are hybrids of diverse parentage and that the species from which they have been produced grow over a wide range of conditions in Africa. So it is not really surprising if

Fig. 14.
Nerine bowdenii.

some of the offspring resemble one parent more than another.

One species, *Nerine bowdenii*, is readily available, never fails to flower and seems to hand on this good quality to its hybrid offspring. Also reliable is the Guernsey lily, *N. sarniensis* and its varieties 'Corusca Major' and 'Fothergillii'. There are probably many others as good, but the experts seem to have selected more for unusual colour or size of bloom than for consistency in performance.

All nerines bear clusters of flowers on bare stems some time between September and November. The leaves begin to appear with the flowers or shortly afterwards and the plants continue to grow slowly all winter, more rapidly in spring and then die down in summer. Some (possibly all) need to be cold, but not frozen, during the February-April period. This, I believe, may be a more critical factor in determining future flowering than warmth and sunshine in July-August, though the two are probably interconnected. The reason for the success of *N. bowdenii* is that it is the hardiest of all, is commonly grown out of doors and any way growers are not afraid to let it get cold in winter and spring. The greenhouse hybrids probably get coddled too much.

Buy nerines in August, grow them in pots in JIP1 with a little extra grit or sand for good drainage. Keep in a sunny place (it does not matter if it is warm or cool) until they have flowered, but when flowers fade keep them cool until the spring. A little frost will not harm *N. bowdenii*, but for others the temperature range should be 5 to 10°C. Keep the soil moist at all times, but water more freely from April to June and during that period feed every 14 days or so with weak liquid fertiliser. From May onwards the more sun and warmth they get the better—a sunny window ledge will suit them well. Repotting is only likely to be necessary every two years and should be done in August. Only the lower half of the bulb should be in the soil.

Good kinds are as follows:

Nerine bowdenii. Rose pink on 2 foot stems, which are even longer in 'Fenwick's Variety' and hybrids such as 'Aurora', 'Hera' and 'Pink Beauty'.

N. flexuosa. Pale pink flowers on 18 inch stems. This retains its foliage more than most and has well developed leaves when in flower. There is a white variety.

N. sarniensis (Guernsey lily). Flowers in various shades of pink and red, also white. Stems 15 to 18 inches. 'Corusca Major' and 'Fothergillii' are both scarlet.

N. undulata. Small, wavy-petalled, pale pink flowers on foot long stems; not showy, but charming.

There are also a great many hybrids sold under 'fancy' names, but these have not yet been properly evaluated to determine the good from the not so good.

Puschkinia.

This looks very much like one of the small scillas, in fact the only species readily available is called *Puschkinia scillioides*, scillioides meaning 'like a scilla'. It is a charming little plant with clusters of small flowers, pale blue with a slight greenish tinge which makes them very distinctive. Cultivation is as for chionodoxa (see p. 16).

Scilla.

The best scillas to grow indoors are the small ones, *Scilla bifolia* and *S. sibirica*, both with deep blue flowers in February-March, and *S. tubergeniana*, with light blue flowers in January-February. All these look lovely in dwarf pots, 9 or 10 bulbs to each $5\frac{1}{2}$ or 6 inch diameter pot. They can be grown in soil or soilless composts and provided they have sufficient light there should be no difficulty in keeping them going for years. Plant them in September with a clear $\frac{1}{2}$ inch between bulbs and $\frac{1}{2}$ inch covering of compost. Subsequently treat in the same way as chionodoxa (p. 16).

Fig. 15.
Scilla tubergeniana.

After flowering either plant out in the garden or leave in the containers until July, then remove the bulbs and store them until September.

Sparaxis (Harlequin Flower).
These are small South African corms related to ixia and requiring similar treatment. The stems are shorter than those of ixia, the flowers upward facing and often richly coloured, coppery red or crimson with a yellow eye surrounded by a nearly black zone, but there are also lighter, white and cream, varieties. All flower in spring and can be grown in south facing windows or other sunny places and then planted outdoors in summer. September is the time to start. When removing the dead foliage it will be found that small cormlets are formed in the lower leaf bases, and if desired can be used to increase the stock, though they will not flower for a couple of years.

Sprekelia (Jacobean Lily, Aztec Lily).
An extraordinary looking, but beautiful Mexican plant with quite large, crimson, spidery flowers carried singly on short stiff stems in May-June. It is grown from a bulb which should be potted in February in JIP1, one bulb in each $4\frac{1}{2}$ inch pot or three bulbs in a 6 inch pot, with the top third of the bulb above soil level. No initial cold period is required. Grow in a

Fig. 16. The Jacobean lily, Sprekelia formosissima.

sunny window, watering sparingly at first, fairly freely when leaves appear, but gradually reducing the water supply in late summer, and keeping almost but not quite dry in winter. Repotting is only likely to be necessary every second or third year, but established bulbs can be fed with weak liquid fertiliser every 10-14 days from May to July.

The only kind is *Sprekelia formosissima*, 9 to 12 inches high.

Sternbergia.
Most people seeing a sternbergia in flower for the first time would probably mistake it for a yellow crocus. In fact sternbergia and crocus are quite unrelated and require different treatment, sternbergia being grown from a bulb, and crocus from a corm. Sternbergias flower in September and October, make their growth from autumn to spring and die down in the summer. They are all sun lovers and this makes them a little difficult to manage indoors unless a really sunny window, sun-room, verandah or something of the kind is available. At least they flower before the spring rush. The leaves are narrow, dark green and shining.

Obtain the bulbs as early as possible, in July if they are available then, certainly not later than early September. Grow them in well-drained pots, preferably in JIP1, and place about 5 bulbs in a 5 inch pot, covering them to a depth of at least $\frac{1}{2}$ inch. Growth will start quickly even out of doors and water will be required all through the autumn, winter and spring in sufficient quantity to keep the compost moist right through. When the leaves eventually die down no more water is needed until the bulbs are re-potted in July.

The two best kinds are *Sternbergia clusiana* and *S. lutea*, both buttercup yellow. *S. clusiana* is a little larger in flower.

Streptanthera.
It is not often that one gets a chance to buy corms of streptanthera, but when they are available they are well worth growing for their very bright colours. They are South African plants, nearly allied to ixia, and requiring identical treatment, but they are much smaller and lack the ixia colour range. *Streptanthera cuprea* is the one most likely to be obtained. It has coppery orange flowers in small sprays on 9 inch stems in late spring or early summer.

Tritonia.
The kind to grow in drained dwarf pots is *Tritonia crocata*. These are charming plants with small sprays of silken textured flowers on slender 9 to 12 inch stems in late spring. There is a fine colour range, from white, cream and yellow to pinks and deep orange, though it is now rare to be able to buy them to colour, and they are either mixed or plain orange. Tritonia is grown from small corms planted in autumn in soil or soilless compost in drained containers. Six or seven of the corms will go easily into a 5 inch diameter dwarf pot. The plants are nearly hardy, only in need of frost protection in winter, and can be kept in a sunny window or some other light place. A few weeks after flowering the foliage starts to die down and then watering should be reduced and by July discontinued until it is time to repot in fresh compost in the autumn. If desired the container can stand outdoors during the summer. Any rain falling on it will do no harm. Protect from mice if necessary.

Tropaeolum.
This is the genus to which the common nasturtium belongs, but that is an annual outside the scope of this book. There are, however, several perennial species with tuberous roots, of which one, *Tropaeolum tricolorum*, is a highly distinctive and attractive plant that can be grown in a sunny window or other really light, frost proof place. It is a small climber with very slender stems, small divided leaves and numerous small, oddly shaped scarlet flowers, each with a nearly black tip. The tubers should be potted in autumn in JIP1 or peat potting compost, one tuber in each 5 inch pot. Water very sparingly until growth appears and then more freely. Push some well branched twigs into the compost or place the pot against a little trellis or other support to which the slender stems can cling. They are so

thin that they are very easily broken. The plants will flower in spring and quite soon after this growth will die down, a signal that watering should be greatly reduced, though I do not think it is wise to let the tuber dry out completely. From June to September the pots can be stood outdoors, and any rain that falls on them will certainly do no harm. In autumn the tubers should be shaken out and replanted in fresh soil.

Fig. 17. The early single yellow tulip 'Mon Tresor'.

Tulipa (Tulip).
These grow very well in drained containers, but are not very satisfactory in bulb fibre in undrained bowls. Tulips are not good bulbs to choose for permanency, as even out of doors they often dwindle away after a few years and this tendency to decline in vigour is even more marked in containers. However, some varieties are much more satisfactory than others in this respect.

There are a great many varieties grouped in classes according to their habit of growth, time of flowering and parentage. The most popular for container growing are the Early Single and Early Double varieties, since they not only flower early but are also relatively short stemmed and therefore self supporting. But later flowering and taller varieties will succeed just as well provided they are supported in some way, e.g. by pushing three or four small canes or sticks into the compost around the edge of each pot and encircling these with a few strands of soft string (fillis). There are also some small species for those who are prepared to look at flowers closely and enjoy the variety of flower shapes and habits of growth which these wild tulips offer.

Specially prepared bulbs are usually available of a few varieties of early single tulips. These have been given controlled heat treatment after very early lifting, followed by cool storage. The temperatures are critical and not the sort of thing an amateur can repeat, but if planted as soon as available the bulbs will flower two or three weeks ahead of untreated bulbs grown in similar conditions, and, of course, much earlier than similar varieties in the garden.

Apart from these prepared bulbs, tulips can be potted at any time from September to November, as convenient, but a better way to ensure a succession of bloom is to choose varieties from early, mid-season and late flowering groups.

Grow in JIP1 or soilless compost, setting the bulbs in this about $\frac{1}{2}$ inch apart (a 6 inch diameter pot will take about seven bulbs), and so that they can be covered to a depth of about $\frac{1}{2}$ inch, still leaving the surface $\frac{1}{2}$ inch below the rim of the pot to prevent water spilling over. All tulip bulbs have one side rather flatter than the rest. If this flat side is placed nearest to the edge of the pot the largest, first leaves to be formed will grow out in that direction, which gives more space in the centre of the pot. This method of placing also allows the bulbs to be packed most economically.

Keep the bulbs cool for the first 12 weeks (9 or 10 for prepared bulbs) during which time they will make their roots and then start shoot growth. They can be kept in the dark during this period, and if outdoors should be in a plunge bed. The ideal temperature is 9°C or slightly less, which is easier to obtain if the pots are covered with moist peat or sand (or indoors with moist newspaper wrappings around the pots) so that the evaporating water lowers the temperature compared with the surrounding air. They must be brought into the light when the flower stems are an inch or so high. At this stage the pots can be brought into ordinary living room conditions provided the light is good, for the better the light the shorter the stems and the healthier the growth. It is particularly important to turn the taller varieties regularly (say a quarter turn daily) as they quickly grow towards the light and the long stems can get very twisted and unmanageable.

The compost must be kept well moist right through from potting time until the leaves begin to yellow in May or June, when watering should decrease and finally stop. The speed with which the foliage dies down is controlled by temperature, a very high temperature setting off the process, even if the pot is then moved to a cooler place. Obviously the longer the period of leaf growth the better the resulting bulb, so this should be borne in mind if it is proposed to try regrowing the bulbs. Tulips make many small bulbs from the big one in most cases, none being big enough to flower the next year. No amount of feeding will get around this, though from the time the flower buds appear a little liquid fertiliser can be added to the the water every 10 days or so to make it worth while planting the bulbs in the garden.

After flowering the foliage gets so untidy that it is desirable to find some place outside to keep the pots, or alternatively the whole ball of compost and bulbs can be tipped out and planted just as it is in the open garden. A sunny spot is best for tulips. If you wish to keep the bulbs in pots indefinitely it is best to choose some of the small species, using dwarf pots. Remember that most of these grow wild in the Middle East and the steppes of Central Asia where sunshine is much stronger and summer temperatures much higher than in Britain, though winters can be very cold, and the growing season short. For this reason tulips have a long season of dormancy from about June until September or even later.

The following are good varieties, arranged in their groups; but there are many more. Specially prepared bulbs are most likely to be available of those marked with an asterisk*.

EARLY SINGLE. 'Bellona', yellow; *'Brilliant Star', scarlet; *'Brilliant Star Maximus', scarlet; *'Christmas Marvel', cherry pink; 'General de Wet', light orange, scented; *'Marshal Joffre', yellow; 'Prince of Austria', orange-red, scented; 'Princess Margaret', pink and white.

EARLY DOUBLE. 'Electra', carmine; *'Golden Ducat', yellow; 'Mr van der Hoef', yellow; 'Peach Blossom', pink; 'Scarlet Cardinal', scarlet; 'Schoonoord', white.

TRIUMPH AND MENDEL (mid-season). 'Apricot Beauty', salmon pink; 'Dutch Princess', orange; 'Garden Party', white edged carmine; 'Kansas', white: 'Merry Widow', red edged white.

FOSTERANA HYBRIDS. 'Cantata', orange scarlet; 'Princeps', scarlet.

KAUFMANNIANA HYBRIDS. 'Heart's Delight', pink and white, yellow base; 'Stresa', yellow and red; 'The First', white flushed carmine.

SPECIES: *Tulipa batalini*, pale yellow, 4 in.; *T. clusiana*, white and cherry red, 12 in.; *T. eichleri*, scarlet, 10 in.; *T. praestans* 'Fusilier', scarlet, several flowers on each 10 in. stem; *T. tarda* (*dasystemon*), yellow and white, several flowers on each 4 in. stem.

Vallota (Scarborough Lily).

I find it strange that the vallota (there is only one kind, *V. speciosa*, sometimes called *V. purpurea*) is so little known and grown. It is a showy plant with scarlet flowers in late August or September, and it is exceptionally easy to grow. Perhaps part of the explanation for its neglect is that, though a true bulb, it does not like to be completely dry or out of soil at any time of the year. So the bulb merchants leave it alone and no one else bothers to take it up.

Because it is never really dormant it does not matter much when it is obtained, but either July or late September, immediately before or after flowering are probably as good times as any. It is a bulb that can be left undisturbed for several years, so a moderately rich soil compost, such as JIP2, is to be preferred to a soilless compost, though the latter can be used with adequate feeding and topping up. Place one bulb in each 4 inch pot and only bury the lower third of the bulb in the compost. It is the natural habit of vallota for the bulb to sit almost on top of the soil. Growth goes on all the year, most actively in spring and early summer when most water is required, but the soil should be kept moist at all times. Feeding can be done with weak liquid fertiliser every 14 days or so from April to June. The bulbs need only be repotted when overcrowded and then can either be moved on in a clump to a larger pot or can be separated and potted singly as at the start.

Vallota likes all the light it can get. A sunny window ledge is the best place for it if it must be grown indoors all the time; but it is sufficiently hardy to stand outside from June until it is about to come into flower in August, and in winter it will be happier in a frost-proof greenhouse than in a room, because the light will be better.

Fig. 12. The Scarborough lily, Vallota purpurea.

Veltheimia.
Here are some more of the less familiar but beautiful South African bulbs. The narrowly tubular flowers are packed in dense heads on a bare stem, rather like kniphofias (red hot pokers) but much smaller and in delicate colours. *Veltheimia capensis* (also known as *V. viridifolia*) is soft pink and *V. glauca* is white and pink. Bulbs should be grown in drained pots in JIP1 or equivalent or a soilless potting compost. Pot in September, one bulb n each 4 inch pot and keep inside in a light place from the outset. Water sparingly at first, fairly freely as growth appears, but gradually dry off in late spring and keep quite dry and in the sunniest place available for a couple of months before repotting in September. Flowers will be produced between November and March and usually last for quite a long time.